AF469478

To Joe Ranft, for the inspiration
and for Eden, Bosco, and Beach

This edition published by Parragon in 2010

Parragon
Queen Street House
4 Queen Street
Bath BA1 1HE, UK

Materials and characters from the movie Cars. Copyright © 2006, 2010, Disney/Pixar.

Disney/Pixar elements © Disney/Pixar, not including underlying vehicles owned by third parties; and, if applicable: Chevrolet Impala are trademarks of General Motors; Dodge, Hudson Hornet are trademarks of Chrysler LLC; Jeep® and the Jeep® grille design are registered trademarks of Chrysler LLC; Ferrari Elements produced under license of Ferrari S.p.A. FERRARI, the PRANCING HORSE device, all associated logos and distinctive designs are property of Ferrari S.p.A. The body designs of the Ferrari cars are protected as Ferrari property under design, trademark and trade dress regulations; Fiat is a trademark of Fiat S.p.A.; Mercury and Model T are registered trademarks of Ford Motor Company; Sarge's rank insignia design used with the approval of the U.S. Army; Volkswagen trademarks, design patents and copyrights are used with the approval of the owner Volkswagen AG.

All rights reserved.

All rights reserved. No part of this publication may be reproduced, stored in a retrieval system or transmitted, in any form or by any means, electronic, mechanical, photocopying, recording or otherwise, without the prior permission of the copyright holder.

ISBN 978-1-4454-5601-0

Printed in China

Written by Kiel Murray
Based on a story by John Lasseter
Illustrations by The Disney Storybook Artists

The morning sun sparkled on the snow in Radiator Springs. Mater the tow truck rushed over to Flo's, carrying a letter.

"Y'all finished your lists to Santa Car, right?" he asked.

"Sure did," replied Flo, the lovely '50s show car.

"Absolutely," said Doc Hudson, the town judge and doctor.

"All right!" exclaimed Mater as he headed for the mailbox.

Mater was just about to mail his letter when he heard a familiar voice.

"Come on, Mater, surely even you know that Santa Car isn't real," said Chick Hicks.

"Next you're gonna tell me that the Easter Buggy don't exist neither," Mater said. Then he dropped his letter into the mailbox.

"What are you doing here, Chick?" asked Lightning McQueen suspiciously.

"Oh, hey, Lightning, didn't see ya there. I just came by to donate to Red's Toy Drive," replied Chick.

Lightning frowned. He was sure that Chick was up to no good.

Just then, Sheriff arrived. "I'm afraid I have some bad news, folks. Petrol stations up and down the route have been robbed. All the fuel has been stolen!"

The townsfolk gasped in shock. "Have they caught the thieves?" asked Doc.

"Not yet," replied Sheriff. "Even the fuel tanks at the post office have been drained!"

“Without fuel, the mail trucks can’t get through! That means the letters won’t get to Santa Car! That means no Christmas!” Mater cried.

Mater immediately drove over to the fuel pump.

“Fill ’er up, Flo. I’ll go to the North Pole and take the letters to Santa Car myself!” he declared.

"I'm tryin'," said Flo, "but there's no fuel!"

Sure enough, Flo's place had been robbed, too!

Mater narrowed his eyes at Chick, who was chuckling with his friends.

Fillmore, the hippie van, whispered to Mater, "Meet me at the dome in five."

When Mater got to the dome, Fillmore filled the tow truck's tank with the last of his Christmas brew. Mater was thrilled.

Fillmore made Mater promise to put his letter on the top of the pile for Santa Car. "Never stop believin', man!" he said.

Back at Flo's, Mater got ready to head out with the letters, but the townsfolk were worried, especially Lightning. He couldn't let Mater go alone. He knew what he had to do.

"Mater, I'm going with you," Lightning said.

"But you can't!" exclaimed Mater. "You don't even have snow tyres!"

"Did somebody say tyres?" said Luigi, the yellow Fiat.

Just as if Lightning were in a race, Guido, the Italian forklift, gave him a quick pit stop.

Then Sarge, the army jeep, added some snow gear of his own. . . .

"Now that's what I call good lookin'! North Pole, here we come!" Mater exclaimed.

"Oh, timing belt, oh, timing belt, how lovely is yer rubber. . . ." Mater sang as he and Lightning started their long journey to the north pole.

Lightning was tired, but Mater's spirits remained high. *"Frosty the snow plow . . ."* he sang. "Come on, buddy, sing it with me!"

Back in town, Sheriff came up with a plan to find the fuel thieves. Luigi and Guido would be scouts. Sally was in charge of maps, and Fillmore would make fuel to keep the search party going.

Moments later, Fillmore discovered that his fuel-making supplies had been stolen! Now he wouldn't be able to fuel the townsfolk for the hunt.

Luckily, Sarge had a plan. "Buck up, soldiers, we'll pool our remaining fuel for Luigi and Guido, and they'll track the thieves," he said.

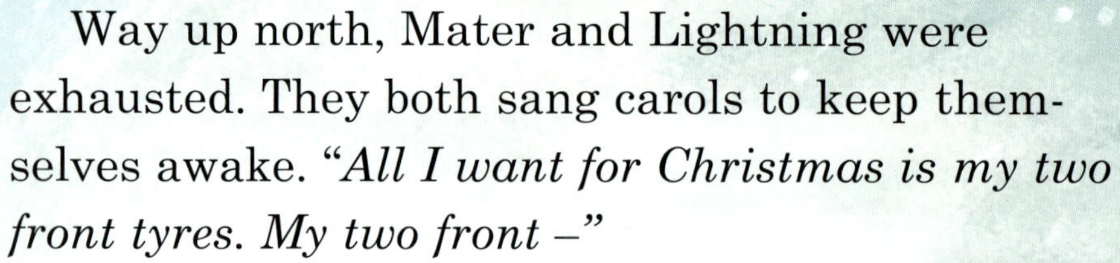

Way up north, Mater and Lightning were exhausted. They both sang carols to keep themselves awake. "*All I want for Christmas is my two front tyres. My two front –*"

BONK!

All of a sudden, Mater hit a candy-striped pole.

"The North Pole! We found it, buddy!" shouted Mater.

It was the North Pole all right, and it was beautiful! Snow-covered garages lined the paths, tiny elf cars bustled about, and in the centre of it all was Santa Car himself.

Mater was overjoyed. Lightning stared in amazement. “Santa Car *is* real!” the race car said.

“Welcome to the North Pole, gentlemen,” said Santa Car.

Santa Car was glad that his new friends had brought their letters all this way, but he had some bad news. “Christmas may be cancelled this year,” he said.

“No Christmas?!” cried Mater.

“The reindeer snowmobiles that fly me around the world have been stolen,” said Santa Car.

Just then, Mater remembered Chick and his friends acting suspiciously at Flo’s. “Chick Hicks took your reindeer!” he cried.

“The reindeer are fed top secret fuel that helps them fly,” said Santa Car.

“The fuel! That’s why he took them!” exclaimed Lightning. “Chick will do anything to win a race.”

"I'd tow you down to Radiator Springs to find yer reindeer, Mr Santa Car, but we'd never make it in time to save Christmas," offered Mater.

But Santa Car had a better idea. He filled Mater's tank with the special flying fuel!

As Mater prepared to tow Santa Car to Radiator Springs, he proudly showed off the antler hat that Mrs Santa Car had knit him for the journey.

Back in Ornament Valley, Luigi and Guido scouted the canyons for the fuel thieves. From a cliff, they spotted Chick and his posse making fuel with Fillmore's supplies! Santa Car's reindeer snowmobiles were there, too!

All of a sudden, two of Chick's pals cornered Guido and Luigi.

"Ha! You're too late, boys!" Chick shouted at Guido and Luigi. "We already reverse-engineered the flying fuel. I'll fly around the track and never lose to Lightning McQueen again! And you know the best part? No more Christmas! No more dirty oil filters in my stocking! If I can't have presents, no one can!"

Suddenly, the air was filled with the sound of jingling bells. Then, Mater soared over the hill, towing Lightning and Santa Car.

Chick raced away, flying just above the ground. Lightning flew after him. Santa Car had filled his tank with the magic fuel back at the North Pole!

Meanwhile, Sheriff and the townsfolk followed Guido's and Luigi's tracks right to Chick's posse. They set Guido, Luigi, and the reindeer free!

Chick was flying fast, but he was no match for Lightning, who knew each turn by heart. As Chick came to a sharp curve, he turned too late, smacked into a giant cactus, and spun out of control.

Doc and Mater joined Lightning on the cliff to take a look at the wreckage.

“Have fun fishin’, Mater,” said Doc. “Tow him straight to jail.”

Back in town, the Radiator Springs gang celebrated the capture of the fuel thieves with Santa Car and his reindeer snowmobiles.

"Well, we better hit the road," said Santa Car. "You know, we could use some help delivering these presents." Mater's eyes lit up.

"What do you say, Mater? Will you help me bring Christmas?" asked Santa Car.

"Sure thing!" yelled Mater. "Let's get 'er done!"

The townsfolk all cheered. Mater had saved Christmas!

Merry Christmas tow all,
and tow all a good night!

First published by Parragon in 2009
Parragon
Queen Street House
4 Queen Street
Bath BA1 1HE, UK

Copyright © 2009 Disney Enterprises, Inc. and Pixar
Cadillac Range background □Inspired by "Cadillac Ranch" by Ant Farm (Lord, Michels and Marquez) © 1974. Disney/Pixar elements © Disney/Pixar; Dodge is a trademark of DaimlerChrysler; Hudson Hornet is a trademark of DaimlerChrysler; Volkswagen trademarks, design patents and copyrights are used with the approval of the owner, Volkswagen AG; H□1 Hummer is a trademark of General Motors; Model T is a registered trademark of General Motors; Fiat is a trademark of Fiat S.p.A.; Mack is a registered trademark of Mac Trucks, Inc.; Mazda Miata is a registered trademark of Mazda Motor Corporation; Kenworth is a trademark of Paccar, Inc.; Chevrolet Impala is a trademark of General Motors; Porsche is a trademark of Porsche; Jeep® is a registered trademark of DaimlerChrysler; Mercury is a registered trademark of Ford Motor Company; Plymouth Superbird is a trademark of DaimlerChrysler; Cadillac Coup de Ville is a trademark of General Motors. Sarge's rank insignia design used with approval of the U.S. Army. Petty marks used by permissiown of Petty Marketing LLC.

All rights reserved. No part of this publication may be reproduced, stored in a retrieval system or transmitted, in any form or by any means, electronic, mechanical, photocopying, recording or otherwise, without the prior permission of the copyright holder.

ISBN 978-1-4454-5601-0
Printed in China

Bath • New York • Singapore • Hong Kong • Cologne • Delhi
Melbourne • Amsterdam • Johannesburg • Auckland • Shenzhen

"Pit stop! Pit stop!" cried Guido as he zoomed over and joined the gang at Flo's café.

The little forklift buzzed with excitement. Would his friend Lightning McQueen win the Piston Cup?

Earlier that week, McQueen had accidentally found himself in Radiator Springs on his way to the tie-breaker race in California. He had to work hard in Radiator Springs, but he also made lots of friends. Now, everyone in Radiator Springs was sad that McQueen was gone . . . but also excited about his big race.

"Do you think he can beat Chick Hicks?" wondered Sally. "I hear Chick is one mean racecar."

"McQueen can beat anybody, I know it!" said Mater. McQueen and Mater had become best friends in a very short time.

Mater believed in McQueen, **one hundred percent!**

htB
htB

They watched a car with a bright green paint job fill the TV screen. It was McQueen's rival, Chick Hicks!

"McQueen? Why should I worry about him?" Chick's voice came through the TV speaker. "He ended up in some rusty little town, playing with tractors and taking Sunday drives. He's not serious about winning. But I am!"

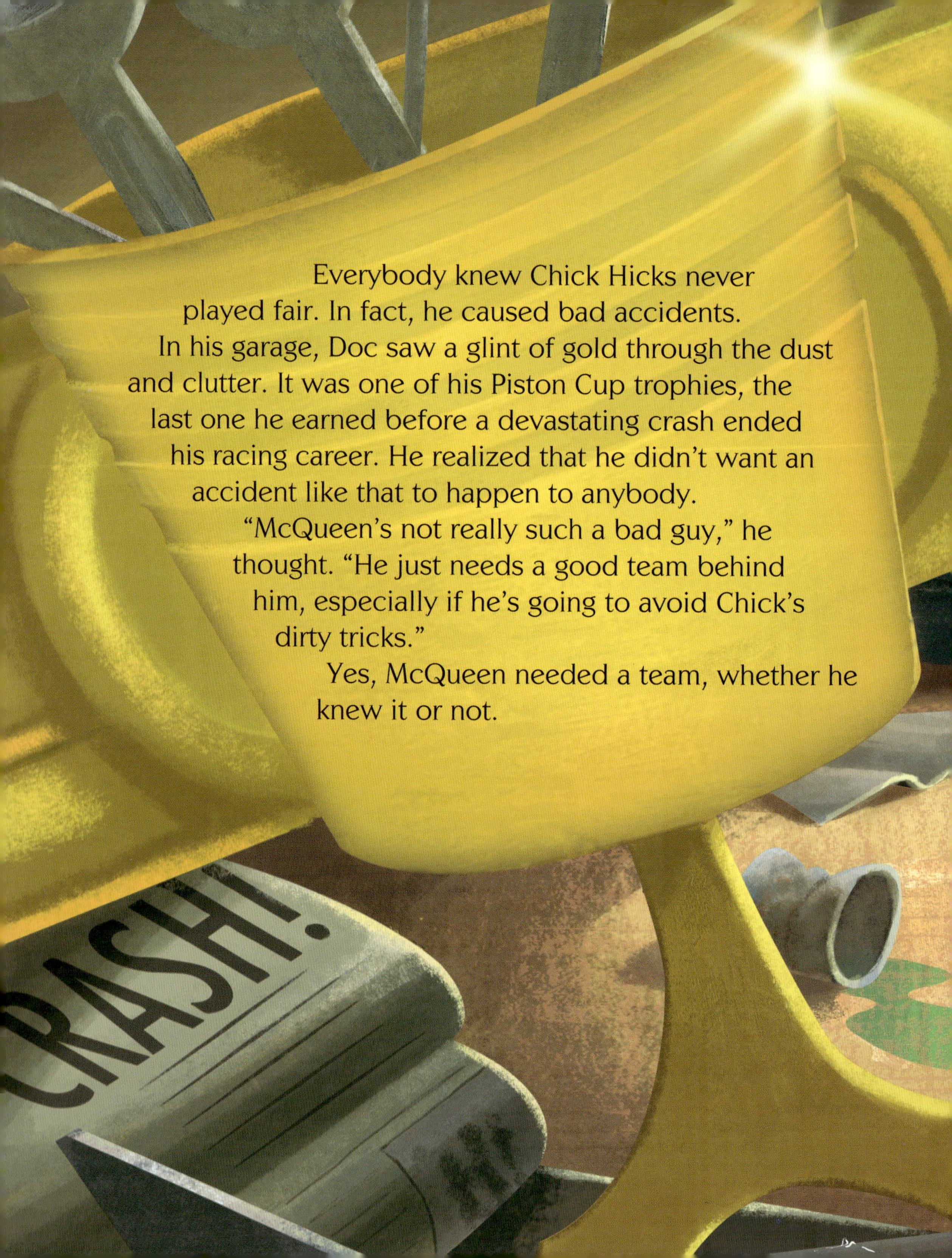

Everybody knew Chick Hicks never played fair. In fact, he caused bad accidents.

In his garage, Doc saw a glint of gold through the dust and clutter. It was one of his Piston Cup trophies, the last one he earned before a devastating crash ended his racing career. He realized that he didn't want an accident like that to happen to anybody.

"McQueen's not really such a bad guy," he thought. "He just needs a good team behind him, especially if he's going to avoid Chick's dirty tricks."

Yes, McQueen needed a team, whether he knew it or not.

“Listen up, everybody,” Doc’s voice boomed down the main street from Flo’s all the way to Sally’s motel. “The rookie needs our help. He’s out there with no pit crew and two tough opponents. I’m not going to let Lightning McQueen lose just because he thinks he can do it all on his own. Who’s with me?”

Everybody was, of course!

Luigi and Guido got to work choosing some tyres. Lightning McQueen would need some good ones.

By morning the crew was inside the stadium. What a feeling it was, to be surrounded by all that excitement! But the Radiator Springs crew had a job to do.

"Pit stop!" said Guido when he saw all the pitties and their tool racks. As soon as Mater unhooked him, he rolled over to a spot to set up.

Sarge took command when he saw the orderly layout of the pit lane and the precise actions of the racing teams.

"You, Flo, over here," he ordered. "Guido, we need the tyres right there."

Ramone had something else in mind, "Hey, Doc! Let me give you a paint job. You gotta let these folks know that you're an important car".

"Not me," said Doc. "Try snazzing-up this pit instead. We need to show off our star car, not me."

Doc drove over to the other side of the track to check out the other crews. But as he neared Chick Hicks' tent he overheard something bad – really bad.

“I’m not gonna let anyone get in the way of me winning that race today,” Chick said to his crew. “If I have to, I’ll make The King and that rookie wipe out so fast their tyres won’t even spin.”

Doc peeked in and saw Chick turn and wink to his crew. “The Cup is mine, boys,” said Chick.

Doc felt his oil heat up. He couldn’t stand for this! It was time to help McQueen, even if it took his last drop of fuel. Could he find McQueen in time to warn him about Chick’s evil plans? Doc returned so fast to the group that he almost overheated.

“This is what friendship is all about,” thought Doc as Ramone finished painting him. “We are all a family.”

And then, as a high-octane boost rushed through him, he climbed the crew-chief platform – with Ramone’s blazing letters freshly painted on his side: Number 51, The Fabulous Hudson Hornet.

51
FABULOUS HUDSON
HORNET

"Look, it's the Hudson Hornet!" cried a car in the stands.

The crowd roared and cheered, louder and louder. Everywhere, Doc saw a sea of flashing headlights and flying antenna balls. They were cheering for him!

Doc was too focused on the upcoming race to smile. But it was clear – Doc Hudson was proud to be back, and it felt good to hear the crowds roaring their approval.

43
95
TWIN H
PISTON CUP

It was all so exciting that no one in the crowd really cared when Chick Hicks was announced the winner of the tiebreaker race.

Instead, they cheered for McQueen as he helped The King cross the finish line. They cheered as they watched McQueen cruise on over to his crew chief, Doc, the Hudson Hornet.

Yes, indeed, the crowd cheered for the real winners of this race: Lightning McQueen and his Radiator Springs family.

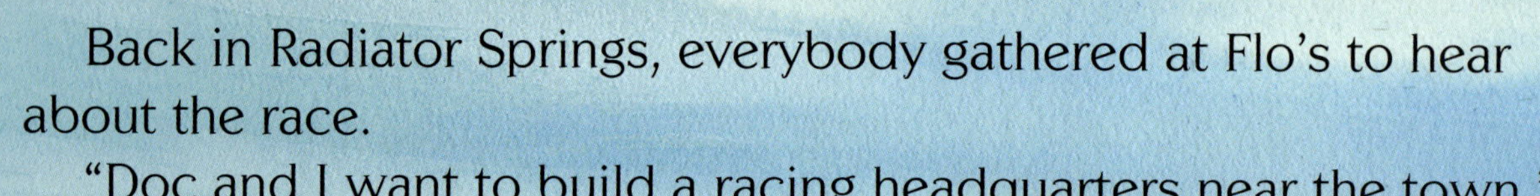

Back in Radiator Springs, everybody gathered at Flo's to hear about the race.

"Doc and I want to build a racing headquarters near the town," McQueen told Sally.

Doc nodded. "It will be a special design – a first-class track that won't spoil our beautiful desert landscape."

"A great idea," said Sally. "And it will put Radiator Springs back on the map."

It wasn't long before Radiator Springs became an international racing sensation. Doc and McQueen sent invitations to race cars all over the world. They came to the town to share tips and techniques on how to become better racers.

WORLD

First published by Parragon in 2011

Parragon
Queen Street House
4 Queen Street
Bath BA1 1HE, UK

Materials and characters from the movie *Cars 2*. Copyright © 2011 Disney/Pixar.

Disney/Pixar elements © Disney/Pixar, not including underlying vehicles owned by third parties; Pacer, and Gremlin are trademarks of Chrysler LLC; Jeep® and the Jeep® grille design are registered trademarks of Chrysler LLC; Maserati logos and model designations are trademarks of Maserati S.p.A. and are used under license; Mercury and Mondeo are registered trademarks of Ford Motor Company; Porsche is a trademark of Porsche; Sarge's rank insignia design used with the approval of the U.S. Army; Volkswagen trademarks, design patents and copyrights are used with the approval of the owner, Volkswagen AG; Bentley is a trademark of Bentley Motors Limited; FIAT and Topolino are trademarks of FIAT S.p.A.; Corvette is a trademark of General Motors; El Dorado is a trademark of General Motors; Chevrolet Impala is a trademark of General Motors; Background inspired by the Cadillac Ranch by Ant Farm (Lord, Michels and Marquez) © 1974.

All rights reserved. No part of this publication may be reproduced, stored in a retrieval system or transmitted, in any form or by any means, electronic, mechanical, photocopying, recording or otherwise, without the prior permission of the copyright holder.

ISBN 978-1-4454-5601-0

Printed in China

MAGICAL STORY

Adapted by Lisa Marsoli

Illustrated by Caroline LaVelle Egan, Scott Tilley, Andrew Phillipson, and Seung Beom Kim

Bath • New York • Singapore • Hong Kong • Cologne • Delhi
Melbourne • Amsterdam • Johannesburg • Auckland • Shenzhen

Finn McMissile, a British secret agent, had slipped onto an oil derrick. He was spying on a spectacled criminal named Professor Z.

Finn hid in the rafters and took photos of a TV camera. He also saw another secret agent who had been crushed into scrap metal!

Back in Radiator Springs, race car Lightning McQueen was at the Wheel Well Restaurant. Miles Axlerod – a former oil tycoon – and Italian race car Francesco Bernoulli were on TV. Axlerod was hosting an international race called the World Grand Prix to introduce his new alternative fuel, Allinol. Lightning agreed to join the race.

Lightning and his pit crew soon arrived in Tokyo for the first race. Mater embarrassed Lightning at the welcome party. He even leaked oil beside Axlerod.

Mater raced off to the bathroom. Inside the automated cubicle, he got poked, prodded and splashed with water!

While Mater was in the cubicle, two members of Professor Z's crew, Grem and Acer, roughed up American Agent Rod "Torque" Redline. When Mater came out of the cubicle, Torque secretly stuck a device underneath Mater.

The following day at the racetrack, Finn and his fellow agent, Holley Shiftwell, kept a close eye on Mater. They thought he was a secret agent, too!

Nearby, Grem and Acer aimed the TV camera at a race car. The camera was a weapon! Seconds later, the car's engine exploded. Some thought Allinol was to blame.

Professor Z's gang then went after Mater in the pits. They wanted the device that the American agent had planted on him.

Just as the bad cars were closing in on Mater, Finn rushed in to the rescue. Mater thought he was watching a karate demonstration!

Since Mater was distracted, he gave Lightning bad racing tips. Lightning ended up losing the race to Francesco!

Lightning blamed Mater. "I lost the race because of you!" he exclaimed.

Mater felt so terrible he decided to go back home. But Finn and Holley whisked him off on a spy mission instead.

Holley removed the planted device from Mater and found a photo of a mysterious, gas-guzzling engine. Mater noticed it had Whitworth bolts, which were very difficult to unscrew.

Meanwhile, Lightning and his team were just outside Porto Corsa, Italy visiting Luigi and Guido's hometown. Lightning talked to Luigi's Uncle Topolino about his fight with Mater.

"Everybody fights now and then, especially best friends," said Uncle Topolino. "But you gotta make up fast."

Holley, Finn and Mater were also on their way to Porto Corsa. Mater had told them the mysterious engine belonged to a Lemon – a car that didn't work right. They soon found out that a secret meeting of Lemons was being held in Porto Corsa. Holley disguised Mater as one of the Lemons' tow trucks so he could sneak into the meeting. She also gave him lots of spy gadgets!

Mater was soon in a room with Professor Z and all the Lemons. Then their "Big Boss", whose identity was hidden, appeared on a TV screen. He told the Lemons that once Allinol was proven dangerous, all cars would go back to using gasoline. Then the Lemons, who owned most of the world's oil, would become wealthy and powerful.

Outside, the second race had begun. Grem and Acer were on a nearby tower with the camera. They aimed it at the race car from Brazil. Her engine suddenly exploded!

Finn raced to the tower to stop Grem and Acer – but a helicopter captured him with a giant magnet!

Back at the race, Lightning crossed the finish line first! He then announced that he would still be using Allinol in the final World Grand Prix race in London.

The Big Boss heard this and gave the order to get rid of Lightning. Mater used his parachute to escape from the meeting. But before he could warn Lightning, Mater was kidnapped by the Lemons. They had captured Holley, too!

Finn, Holley and Mater were tied up inside the clockworks of Big Bentley in London. Mater finally convinced Finn and Holley that he wasn't a spy.

After the final race began, Grem and Acer told Mater they had planted a bomb inside Lightning's pit. As soon as the Lemons left, Mater escaped, racing to save his best friend.

Minutes later, Holley and Finn escaped, too. They soon discovered the Lemons had actually planted the bomb on Mater! Finn radioed the tow truck to tell him, but Mater was already in the pits.

"Stay away from me!" Mater warned Lightning.

But Lightning still raced forwards to see his best friend!

Meanwhile, Professor Z tried to escape on a combat ship, but Finn stopped him. He tied the Professor up in cables and brought him to Holley, Mater and Lightning.

Then Guido tried to remove the bomb on Mater, but he couldn't unscrew the bolts. Suddenly, everything made sense to Mater. He knew who the Big Boss was!

Mater flew with Lightning to Buckingham Palace. Mater told everyone that Axlerod was the Big Boss! Mater had figured it out because the bolts on the bomb were the same Whitworth bolts from the old British engine in the photo. The engine belonged to Axlerod. He was the biggest Lemon of all! Axlerod deactivated the bomb and everyone was saved.

The Queen thanked Mater by making him a knight!

Not long after Lightning got back home, he decided to hold his own "Radiator Springs Grand Prix". He invited all the international race cars. The whole town turned up for the race.

Finn and Holley showed up, too. They had come to invite Mater on their next mission. Mater politely turned them down. But he did take his spy gadgets for one last spin! Mater activated his rockets and blasted off down the racetrack, right beside his speedy best friend.

grand prix
00:00
00
一方通行カフェ
レンチ
そく堂
入口
ゴーゴー
RIDE
アリノール
WORLD grand PRIX